> Challenges are what make life interesting and overcoming
> them is what makes life meaningful.
> JOSHUA J. MARINE

DATE:

Definiteness of purpose is the starting point of all achievement.
W. CLEMENT STONE

Don't wait. The time will never be just right.
NAPOLEON HILL

DATE:

DATE: _______________________

Success is going from failure to failure without losing your enthusiasm.
WINSTON CHURCHILL

Eighty percent of success is showing up.
WOODY ALLEN

DATE: _______________

DATE:

Whatever the mind of man can conceive and believe, it can achieve.
NAPOLEON HILL

DATE: _______________

An unexamined life is not worth living.
SOCRATES

The journey of a thousand miles begins with one step.
LAO TZU

I can't change the direction of the wind,
but I can adjust my sails to always reach my destination.
JIMMY DEAN

Strive not to be a success, but rather to be of value.
ALBERT EINSTEIN

DATE:

The best preparation for tomorrow is doing your best today.
H. JACKSON BROWN JR

The power of imagination makes us infinite.
JOHN MUIR

> Two roads diverged in a wood, and I - I took the one
> less traveled by, And that has made all the difference.
> ROBERT FROST

Dream big and dare to fail.
NORMAN VAUGHAN

DATE: _______________________

I attribute my success to this: I never gave or took any excuse.
FLORENCE NIGHTINGALE

DATE: ___________________

You miss 100% of the shots you don't take.
WAYNE GRETZKY

DATE:

Start by doing what's necessary; then do what's possible;
and suddenly you are doing the impossible.
FRANCIS OF ASSISI

It is never too late to be what you might have been.
GEORGE ELIOT

DATE: _______________

DATE:

Definiteness of purpose is the starting point of all achievement.
W. CLEMENT STONE

Life is what happens to you while you're busy making other plans.
JOHN LENNON

DATE:

We become what we think about.
EARL NIGHTINGALE

DATE: ___________________

Perfection is not attainable, but if we chase
perfection we can catch excellence.
VINCE LOMBARDI

You must be the change you wish to see in the world.
GANDHI

DATE:

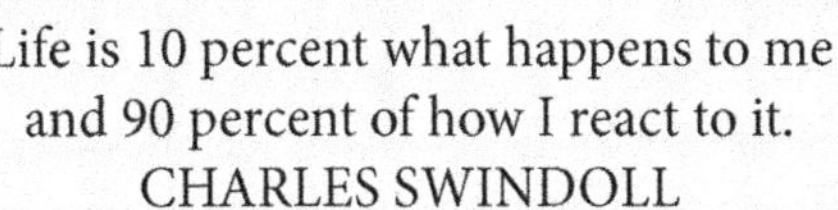

Life is 10 percent what happens to me
and 90 percent of how I react to it.
CHARLES SWINDOLL

Your imagination is your preview of life's coming attractions.
ALBERT EINSTEIN

> The most common way people give up their
> power is by thinking they don't have any.
> ALICE WALKER

Even if you fall on your face, you're still moving forward.
VICTOR KIAM

DATE: _______________________

The dreamers are the saviors of the world.
JAMES ALLEN

DATE:

Try to be a rainbow in someone's cloud.
MAYA ANGELOU

DATE:

A year from now you may wish you had started today.
KAREN LAMB

DATE: ______________________

> Very often a change of self is needed more than a change of scene.
> ARTHUR CHRISTOPHER BENSON

DATE: ______________________

Change your thoughts and you change your world.
NORMAN VINCENT PEALE

DATE: _______________

Keep your face to the sunshine and you can never see the shadow.
HELEN KELLER

DATE:

Every child is an artist. The problem is how
to remain an artist once he grows up.
PABLO PICASSO

If you can't outplay them, outwork them.
BEN HOGAN

You can never cross the ocean until you have
the courage to lose sight of the shore.
CHRISTOPHER COLUMBUS

DATE: ______________________

Life shrinks or expands in proportion to one's courage.
ANAIS NIN

DATE:

If you hear a voice within you say 'you cannot paint,'
then by all means paint and that voice will be silenced.
VINCENT VAN GOGH

Ask and it will be given to you; search, and you will find;
knock and the door will be opened for you.
JESUS

If there is no struggle, there is no progress.
FREDERICK DOUGLASS

DATE:

We know what we are, but know not what we may be.
WILLIAM SHAKESPEARE

The only person you are destined to become
is the person you decide to be.
RALPH WALDO EMERSON

> The more I want to get something done, the less I call it work.
> RICHARD BACH

DATE:

Go confidently in the direction of your dreams.
Live the life you have imagined.
HENRY DAVID THOREAU

DATE: _______________________

> Everything you've ever wanted is on the other side of fear.
> GEORGE ADDAIR

If you aren't going all the way, why go at all?
JOE NAMATH

DATE: _______________________

> Start where you are. Use what you have. Do what you can.
> ARTHUR ASHE

Fall seven times and stand up eight.
JAPANESE PROVERB

What we fear doing most is usually what we most need to do.
TIM FERRISS

When I let go of what I am, I become what I might be.
LAO TZU

DATE:

> The difference between ordinary and extraordinary is that little extra.
> JIMMY JOHNSON

If you want to lift yourself up, lift up someone else.
BOOKER T. WASHINGTON

DATE:

Don't count the days, make the days count.
MUHAMMAD ALI

You take your life in your own hands, and what happens?
A terrible thing, no one to blame.
ERICA JONG

I have learned over the years that when one's
mind is made up, this diminishes fear.
ROSA PARKS

Every moment is a fresh beginning.
T.S. ELIOT

DATE: ___________________

It does not matter how slowly you go as long as you do not stop.
CONFUCIUS

DATE: ____________________

Remember that not getting what you want is
sometimes a wonderful stroke of luck.
DALAI LAMA

DATE: _______________________

You may be disappointed if you fail,
but you are doomed if you don't try.
BEVERLY SILLS

DATE: _____________________

If you do what you've always done,
you'll get what you've always gotten.
TONY ROBBINS

A person who never made a mistake never tried anything new.
ALBERT EINSTEIN

DATE: _______________

The person who says it cannot be done should
not interrupt the person who is doing it.
CHINESE PROVERB

DATE: _______________________

Just keep going. Everybody gets better if they keep at it.
TED WILLIAMS

Made in the USA
Monee, IL
07 July 2026

56552042R00085